It's time to FIGHT BACK

The Opticians Essential Guide to Growing an Independent Practice

By
Richard Pakey, FBDO
With Paul Green

Published by Independent Practice Growth UK

www.opticiansmarketing.co.uk

INDEPENDENT PRACTICE GROWTH UK

Supporting opticians growing,
marketing and selling practices

First published in Great Britain in 2011 by
Independent Practice Growth UK
Part of Publicity Heaven Ltd
1 The Old Dairy
Knuston Home Farm
Irchester
Northants
NN29 7EX

08452 303049
www.opticiansmarketing.co.uk
hello@opticiansmarketing.co.uk

ISBN 978-0-9562952-1-7

Printed by the MPG Books Group in the UK

For my wife, Julia,

Who has supported me in every aspect of my life and who then gave us the greatest gift, our son Sam

Richard Pakey
February 2011

How to work less, have fewer clients and less stress – yet make significantly more money from your practice over the next 12 months

It's been a really tough couple of years to be an independent optician, hasn't it?

The multiples are being much more aggressive with their marketing, enticing clients with offers that are frankly hard to match. And they are scarily efficient at getting clients to stay loyal and return year after year.

Online glasses websites have added further pressure, including the phenomenon of the "prescription-only" patient costing your practice money.

Never before have people in the UK considered eye care to be a commodity product in the way they do now. Which has made it harder for opticians to offer an excellent and quality service and still operate a highly profitable business.

Add in the worst recession in living memory, and there are lots of opticians I know who have really struggled over the last year. I predict some will be forced to lose staff, or maybe even close their practices in the near future.

Yet against this background, I've seen my two practices grow by **18%** over the last year.

So, am I a better optician than you? Or smarter? Better educated?

No, I'm absolutely not! The only thing that's different about me is the way I think about my practices, and the way I run them.

I'm not telling you this to boast. I'm telling my story because I want to help you.

You see, I realised a few years ago that my practices are there for me, and not the other way round! Many independent opticians are slaves to their business. They are there 10 hours a day seeing clients, before they even start to look at the important things that keep a practice running well, such as good marketing, positive finances, and efficient operations.

Don't get me wrong, I work long hours building up my practices too. But every day the majority of my time is invested in growing my business, not working in it.

This is one of the 12 key areas of running a successful opticians practice. I've been interviewing a number of other opticians and working closely with PR and marketing expert Paul Green to identify these areas.

In this book I'm going to tell you what they are and show you how you can significantly improve them in your business.

I'm passionate about helping this industry thrive over the next decade. It will be devastating if independent opticians start to go out of business, leaving the multiples to deliver all the eye care in this country. Don't get me wrong, there is a place for the multiples. But we need a healthy balance of the two.

So I decided to create Independent Practice Growth UK to help independent opticians fight back.

Now, rather than feel frustrated when I meet another optician who is struggling with their practice, I am able to offer them significant help in a formal way.

If the information in this book proves invaluable to your practice, please let me know. You can email me any time: richard@opticiansmarketing.co.uk

And I highly recommend you join me at a free opticians marketing and business growth seminar in the near future. You can see full details at the back of the book.

Here's to your future success.

Richard Pakey

Richard Pakey
Owner of two independent opticians practices
And **co-founder** of Independent Practice Growth UK

The 12 key areas of running a successful opticians practice

I became an optician purely by chance, and I'm glad I did.

At the age of 19 I was working as an electrical labourer, mostly outdoors, and was fed up going home every day wet and dirty. I wanted a nice cosy office job instead! And when I saw one advertised at Vision Express, where I could work nine to five and wear a suit, I went for it, despite knowing nothing about optics.

This was in 1998 when I became a trainee lab technician for about £6,000 a year. I really enjoyed the work and must have shown some promise, as within three months I'd been made lab manager. Then within 18 months I was assistant store manager, and by the age of 21 I was area manager looking after three practices within a franchise area.

As you can imagine this was a pretty frantic time. I knew I loved working in the industry, and while I was pleased with my progress, I realised there was a danger I would only ever know the Vision Express way. I'd been visiting independent stores in my area to see how they differed, and realised there was actually more opportunity there.

So I quit Vision Express, and took my girlfriend (now my wife) travelling.

We went to Australia... and stopped there for six months so I could study the optical industry there. I realised the country was years behind the UK and that created huge opportunity. It's no surprise to me that Specsavers is so dominant there now.

Back to the UK, where an agency was introducing me to independent practices that would train me. I walked into one practice that was still operating under the old rules. There was a very small reception area with a receptionist but no frames on display. Nothing in the windows. It was dark and dingy with only a tenth of the space used for retail; the rest for office space.

Most 22-year-olds would have run a mile! But I realised this would be a fantastic opportunity. I didn't know what, but something clicked in my mind and I realised I wanted to be there. They clearly wanted me too. This was 1999, and they took me on as a lab manager/ trainee dispensing optician at £35,000 a year. I was even driving a brand-new company BMW which I'd specced myself.

The owners had had the practice for about 12 years already and had vague retirement plans. I was able to say to them "look if I was here, this is what I'd like to do with this business" which really opened their eyes.

Updating the practice was fun, if not easy. The office space had to be turned over to retail. It had to look like an opticians and be inviting for clients. And we needed to bring in brands.

Gucci was very big in the nineties and I remember debating with my boss over our first £2,000 order for frames. "Richard," he told me, "if we don't sell those frames within a month then you'll be buying them with your final pay cheque before you leave!"

Of course the Gucci glasses went on to be our best line for the next four years.

Financially, the practice was doing OK at the time, turning over the average for a practice of its size. Since buying it from the owners in 2005, **turnover has trebled and profits doubled in real terms.**

And that was driven by necessity. The costs of the business had risen dramatically to cover the business loan repayments. So we needed to increase turnover, fairly significantly and rapidly. One of the ways we did that was by introducing brands in a big way.

If you're not really sure about the power of brands, let me tell you that it is virtually impossible to grow a successful independent opticians practice without them. The right brand is far bigger and more lucrative than your practice's brand.

If you bring in a brand like Prada, that will mean far more to a certain group of people than the name of your practice. Prada spends millions of pounds every year building up a willingness in clients to buy their products at extremely premium prices. Why wouldn't you want the benefit of that – and the dozens of other premium brands – within your business?

The business's growth was rapid. All of a sudden, the ideas that had built up over the years could be tried out. I was lucky to have a very good practice manager in Shane, who was as ambitious as I was. In fact, all the staff were exceptionally receptive to it, because they were also getting to a point where they were looking for change. A big reason the practice has grown as it has is down to the high quality of the staff. We've been very lucky to keep every single one since the purchase.

From 2005 to **today** the practice has achieved double digit growth every year. The business as a whole has continued to see similar growth thanks to the opening of the second practice.

Despite that practice being based in a village with a population of only 3,500 people, it returned a profit within nine months. My older practice examines six days per week; the new one just one day a week. Yet it returns half the profit that my 23 year old practice returns. That's because we were able to design it to be that profitable from scratch.

Working with PR and marketing expert Paul Green, I have spent several months analysing the two practices to see exactly what it is that makes them so successful, at a time when many other opticians are struggling.

There are 12 key areas to running a successful opticians practice, split into three distinct categories:

Sales and marketing for opticians
1) Create a consistent and controllable flow of new leads, referrals, and footfall to your business
2) Improve your website to get more traffic, then convert it into new client enquiries
3) Persuade clients to visit more often, and spend more every time they visit

How to stop the multiples being a threat to your business
4) End the problem of prescription-only clients
5) Sell more commodity products without competing on price
6) Use your independence as a unique marketing advantage and differentiator
7) Dominate your local media without spending a penny on advertising
8) Create systems that make clients feel valued at every touchpoint - automatically

Grow your practice and sell it
9) Ensure your business thrives with operational excellence
10) Why you must stop seeing clients yourself, and lose some of them by increasing your prices
11) Create a highly positive cashflow
12) Prepare your business for a highly profitable exit

Let's look at the 12 different areas in more detail.

Sales and marketing for opticians

1) Create a consistent and controllable flow of new leads, referrals, and footfall to your business

So it's nine o'clock in the morning, you're looking at your diary and you see five or six spaces. You don't have the kind of practice where there is more demand for appointments than supply. It's going to be another quiet day, isn't it?

This is a classic sign of a reactive practice. You have sent out your reminders; a percentage of those people have called to book their appointment, and... that's it. The ones who don't call become lapsed clients. And there are hundreds of potential new clients out there who are picking other practices, simply because your marketing doesn't reach them.

I say you need a **proactive practice.**

A proactive practice never lets an active client lapse. If they want to go somewhere else, they have to make a conscious decision to do so! Because they hear from you regularly, so they don't have chance to "forget" who their optician is, or be tempted to look elsewhere.

The proactive practice also has a system to create a consistent and controllable flow of new clients into the business I make no apology for using the word "client" over "patient" by the way. When you talk about clients you realise you are primarily running a business, not a medical service.

One of the simplest and most reliable ways to drive new business is to ask for referrals. But this can't be done in a higgledy piggledy way; it needs to be a formal process that every member of your team adheres to. The best time to ask a client for a referral is at the point they are happiest with you – when you have just dispensed them with some new glasses.

Remember that like refers like. If you want more reliable, higher spending clients, then ask your more reliable, higher spending clients who they think would benefit from the kind of service they have just enjoyed.

What about paid-for marketing? Sadly, most opticians waste their marketing money on adverts that don't work. Putting an advert into a directory or magazine that features pictures of beautiful people in glasses along with your logo and phone number simply will not generate business for your practice!

The key to advertising that generates business is something called direct response marketing. You want people who see your advert to immediately contact your business, preferably by visiting your website. There, they should be encouraged to give you their contact details in return for some kind of golden carrot, such as a discount on their frames, or better still, educational information about eye tests and choosing frames.

People who respond to these kinds of advert are much more likely to go on to become great clients for your business, because they are putting their hand up and declaring themselves to be a great prospect.

This mix of permission marketing and educational marketing also gives you a large list of prospects to market to. When people give you their contact details they are putting YOU in charge of the marketing. You don't have to hope they will remember your practice or will bookmark the website address (most people don't do that any more).

Instead you can direct market to them. You are in control of the relationship. OK, you can't make people book an appointment before they are ready, but you can make sure that the second they are ready to see an optician, it's you that they choose.

The third form of marketing you should rely on to build your practice is PR. Getting free publicity in the media read and listened to by your potential clients is a very powerful thing indeed (especially when combined with the direct response marketing described above).

Journalists are desperate for good stories every day, and as an optician, they hold you in higher regard than most business people. My colleague Paul Green was a journalist for 13 years working in newspapers and radio stations. He was hardly ever approached by opticians with story suggestions, until just before major awareness campaigns such as National Eye Health Week. Then they all turned up at once!

There are massive opportunities for your business to be featured in your local media simply by sending high quality, well written press releases, and ensuring you meet a few basic rules to give journalists exactly what they want, when they need it. More on this later.

2) Improve your website to get more traffic, then convert it into new client enquiries

How much traffic does your website get, and how well does that traffic convert into new enquiries?

Most opticians don't know the answer to this because they don't track what's happening on their website. I know that at least half of the new enquiries in my practices come directly from the website, and exactly what return on investment I get from every £1 invested in driving web traffic.

You need to install simple but powerful software such as Google Analytics, so you can track exactly how many people are visiting your website, and know exactly what they are doing when they are there.

Where are they coming from? How many bounce (land on your website then hit the back button)? What pages do they visit? Where do they exit the site?

Your website has three important functions:

1) **Position your business correctly:** To fight the multiples you must be seen as the local expert. People judge a business by the home page of its website alone. A cheap or confusing website could be damaging your business. Clients also respond well when they see you have a wide variety of brands they have heard of

2) **Generate leads:** Every page of your site should have data capture so you can find out who is visiting and then stay in touch with them. Putting a box that says "sign up for our newsletter" is the least effective thing you can do. You need an

effective golden carrot to dangle in front of visitors, as described above. To give you a guide, at least half of all the people who visit your site for the first time can be persuaded to give their email address and phone number, along with their permission to be contacted

3) **Pre-frame and upsell existing clients:** Those clients who are proactive are likely to visit your website to get your contact details, before they book an appointment. And you can't waste that opportunity to position your business and set out what they can buy from you. Your latest brands and frames must be highlighted using benefit-driven copy (the marketing name for content). And you can take the opportunity to give them some kind of personalised offer voucher, which will encourage them to buy more when they visit for their appointment. This kind of approach can also be used to target specific clients who aren't so time-sensitive, and try to persuade them to book their appointment at a less popular time

To make this happen you need a traffic generation strategy. That means at least five, ideally ten different ways of driving traffic to your site. Reliable methods that work well for opticians include pay per click (Google AdWords); search engine optimisation (SEO); search engine marketing (there is a difference); free publicity; and direct response advertising (for me, inserts in publications often outperform adverts, especially if the inserts are of a very high quality).

3) Persuade clients to visit more often, and spend more every time they visit

There are only three ways to grow your practice:
1) Get more clients
2) Get those clients to purchase more often
3) Persuade clients to visit more often, and spend more every time they visit

Most opticians focus almost exclusively on the first method. Yet often, the fastest source of new revenue in a practice is with the other two.

When I bought my first practice clients were returning on average once every three years. In a short space of time we got that down to about two years. But I want it to be every six months.

That's not going to be as difficult as you'd think. There are a number of reasons to get clients to come back to your practice, and not just for an eye test or to buy frames. You could book everyone who purchases new frames in for a complimentary six month frame check.

Once someone is sitting in front of you, you are building a relationship with them, and they are much more likely to buy something else. You check their lenses and adjust their frames as needed. Look for any repairs that need to be done. Check their eye solutions still match their lifestyle. Do they need sunglasses, or specialist swimming goggles?

I know that some opticians (and especially optometrists) feel uncomfortable selling things to people. Some have said to me that they pride themselves on not selling to their clients; that they are there to keep their clients' eyes healthy and if people want to buy frames or contacts, that's their choice. They're not going to suggest it.

I'm sorry, but that's a very old fashioned way to look at a practice. Clients want to know what their options are and how you can help them. If they didn't want to buy something, they wouldn't! But you offer them prescription goggles that help them enjoy their weekly swim more, and you become the hero. You both benefit.

It's vital to educate your clients about what you sell; the brands you offer; and the benefits of using them. And you must do this **BEFORE** they sit in the chair! People who are pre-educated make better clients, buy more products; and feel happier with their purchase afterwards.

The reality is that you have a business, and that business needs clients who spend money, generating a profit. Profits are good. They allow you to invest in the business's infrastructure, in more marketing, and – most importantly of all – in giving you a better lifestyle.

You might not want to drive around in an Aston Martin. But maybe you would prefer to spend more time with your family or pursuing a favourite hobby. A profitable practice helps you achieve this. And the most profitable practices are those that focus on sales and marketing.

How to stop the multiples being a threat to your business

4) End the problem of prescription-only clients

The disruption that Jamie Murray Wells has created with Glasses Direct is welcome, in my opinion. Because it's forcing independent opticians to move away from clinical-based practices, and decide what kind of clients they would really like to work with.

None of us want the prescription-only client. I always tell my staff that it would be cheaper for us to give them a £50 note than actually get them in the chair! Send them to the multiples I say – if they want to compete purely on price... then let them and the glasses websites fight to the death.

Over the next few years I am convinced we are going to see PCT fees start to shrink. It costs around £150 an hour to run the average practice. If you are being paid £20 odd for a 30 minute appointment that costs you £75 to deliver, there's a big problem. **You simply can't afford to see prescription-only clients.**

It's in our marketing that we start the process of weeding these people out. Prescription-only clients are very price-sensitive. Which is why excellent positioning and the use of premium brands is so important. People who intend to take their prescription to a glasses website look for an appointment that costs the least and will give them the minimum amount of hassle.

My staff are the next line of defence. If a potential client displays some of the warning signs at the point of booking an appointment, my team ask them outright if they are intending to do this. If they are, we tell them it will be cheaper and easier to visit the multiple down the road!

(If you'd have told me a few years ago that I'd be referring business to the multiples...!)

For those that do get through and sit in the chair, we identify them early then offer them a "secret" remarkably-priced entry level campaign, not available to normal clients. It demonstrates that by buying from the practice, they can save two to three times what they would save online. Plus they avoid the risk of buying online. This is not always highly profitable, but at least helps to subsidise the cost of the eye exam.

5) Sell more commodity products without competing on price

The number one factor in the rapid growth of my practices has been selling premium commodity products to clients. And this while the internet has risen as a source of the cheapest glasses possible.

The reason we have done so well is that we are not dealing with price-sensitive people, and we have "hidden" the cost of glasses in an overall bundle of services.

Most of our clients don't care that they can get their frames a little cheaper online. They care more about getting the right health care; about having their frames fitted properly; and being treated like a valued client.

They like the **"pomp and circumstance"** of being dealt with by an optician. Of being surrounded by machinery, and an expert that they have come to know and trust sitting chatting with them about their health.

The internet is not appealing to them. Because frames bought on the internet are cheap. Cheap is a bad word for these clients. They don't buy cheap; they buy the best that they can afford, because they are educated that their eyes are very important and they want to look after them (plus feel great when they buy the latest branded frames).

Let me be totally clear about this: **There is no space at the bottom of the market for independent opticians.** Let the multiples fight over that space. In fact, beware of sitting in the middle of the market, as the multiples are greedily eyeing that up too. To be a successful practice that will thrive over the next few years, you need to focus on the top end of the market.

You also need to put your prices up. My practices' prices go up every year. Each time this happens I lose a few clients (mostly the ones I didn't want anyway) and my profits rise. We make more money seeing fewer people who buy more. Incredible!

It's actually known as the multiplier effect. Here's how to grow your business by 33% over the next 12 months:

- You get 10% more clients.
- You get them to return 10% more frequently than they normally do.
- You get them to spend 10% more every time they visit.

Just improving each of these three areas by 10% combines to create a 33% increase in revenue for your business.

Can you see how achieving double digit growth in your business is possible, no matter where you start from?

6) Use your independence as a unique marketing advantage and differentiator

I suspect that in the next few years, a number of independent opticians will make a decision to give up the struggle and buy into a multiple franchise.

The reality is; only the franchisor will benefit from that in the long term. Because the best sites in every town and city are gone. The multiples and other independents already have them.

You might see that being the only independent on the High Street, surrounded by multiples, is a disadvantage. Not at all. I'd actually say that you are in an advantageous position.

Because clients know which practices are part of a chain and which are not. And many people see a small standalone practice as a good thing. In fact, the premium clients you really want are likely to see it as a desirable quality.

They may perceive that an owner-managed practice is more likely to have better customer service; to look after clients better; and to care more about healthcare. When someone's name is above the door there is a perception that they will do a better, higher quality job than someone who operates under a national brand.

We know of course that most of the multiples do just as good a job as we do. But marketing is not about the reality of your practice, it's about the perception. If someone thinks that your practice is high quality, then it is. Simple as that. Perception is reality.

Now I'm not saying that your service and the eye healthcare you deliver is not important. It's critical (more on that later). The point I'm trying to make is that it doesn't matter how good or bad your service actually is – it's how good or bad people **PERCEIVE** it to be.

Perception is driven by excellent positioning and consistent marketing messages. You can't afford to hide away and hope that people will just realise your practice is locally-owned, and independent.

The sad reality is that no-one cares about your practice as much as you do. People don't sit at home thinking about their optician. They don't obsess over the practice or the website like you might. For everyone except opticians, picking an optician is a 3 minute exercise!

This is why you need to keep pushing your position as the local premium eye healthcare expert. And it's why you can't afford to ever switch off your marketing. You need to be pushing your position 365 days a year; using automated and outsourced marketing methods wherever you can.

You should also totally ignore how the multiples are marketing themselves. Who cares if their marketing is all about the price. Leave them to fight amongst themselves for the price-sensitive clients, while you feast on the premium clients who visit more often and spend more.

7) Dominate your local media without spending a penny on advertising

Most opticians waste their marketing spend on adverts that simply don't work. Which is a real shame, as by using PR (public relations) instead, they could get journalists effectively recommending their business at a fraction of the cost.

There are three key differences between advertising and public relations. The first and most obvious is the cost. You pay for advertising, whereas publicity is free (if you have to pay for it, then it's called an advertorial).

But the real differences are in credibility and control. Adverts have very high levels of control, as when you pay for space in a newspaper, magazine or on a radio station, you can say virtually anything you like within a few advertising laws. However adverts have very low credibility. People know an advert when they see one, and know you have full control.

Free publicity is exactly the opposite. You cannot control what a journalist says about your practice (you can heavily influence what journalists write, but you don't get the final approval). However if they write that you are the local eyecare expert, then people will believe them. Journalists have amazing influence.

As opticians, we are lucky that journalists don't view us as everyday business owners. In their minds we are put together with doctors and dentists as healthcare providers. This is a good thing. Because journalists hate giving free advertising to businesses. It's one of the main reasons that other businesses fail to get featured in their local media.

Because we're different we can get publicity where normal businesses can't. But we still need to give journalists what they want. They don't want to be bombarded with rubbish press releases. They certainly don't want to go out to lunch with you! Instead they just want relevant, interesting story suggestions, in the form of well written, targeted and relevant press releases.

Some journalists – radio presenters in particular – also respond well to free gifts. My colleague Paul Green spent nine years as a commercial radio presenter. During that time he didn't pay for a single CD, DVD or cinema ticket. He ate free in dozens of restaurants and even attended big concerts at no cost. Guess which businesses got mentioned on his radio show!

But you need to be extremely careful how you approach the local media with freebies, and exactly what you offer. It's all too easy to give a radio presenter hundreds of pounds worth of free frames and get absolutely nothing back in return. You also have to be extremely careful that the media title does not feel you have deliberately dropped paid advertising in favour of a free publicity approach. Most local newspapers and radio stations have small advertising and editorial teams who talk often. They will "punish" a practice that they see is hurting their revenue streams.

There are a number of key PR strategies that will generate valuable and credible publicity for your practice in the right way, avoiding the common pitfalls.

8) Create systems that make clients feel valued at every touchpoint - automatically

I try very hard not to spend more than one day a week at each of my practices. The other three days are invested in working ON my business as opposed to IN it. This means the most important activities that will move the business forward.

I have meetings, I work on projects, and I develop marketing ideas. The reason I can do this – confident that my practices will not fall over without me – is because I have great staff, who operate great systems.

It's the systems which are the most important. Staff come and eventually they go. But the systems remain year after year. It's the systems which create the consistent experience clients come to expect every time they deal with your practice.

If they were served with a cup of tea the first time they visited for an appointment, you will irritate them by not offering a cuppa when they return. Whether it's good service or bad, clients expect consistency.

There are hard systems, soft systems, automated systems and information systems.

Hard systems don't need any work to make things happen a certain way. For example, if it's important to you that your reception is warm, then a thermostat set to the desired temperature is a hard system. It doesn't require human intervention to turn the heating on and keep the reception warm.

A soft system dictates the way you want your staff to act. Let's say you wanted every single client arriving at the practice to have their contact details checked; be given a health questionnaire and be served a cup of tea. You'd put these items into a checklist and make it a rule that the receptionist completed the checklist for every client.

Simple but effective. Because it makes it easy to improve your business. As you make changes you add items to the checklist, then simply manage by systems. If the receptionist is completing the checklist correctly each time, then they are doing their job properly. And importantly, that means they are running the business exactly how you want them to.

Finally you have automated systems. I use these mostly for marketing. For example, all marketing messages from my practices are controlled by a powerful piece of web-based software called Infusionsoft.

You tell it about your prospects (including what kind of prospect they are), and it sends them relevant emails automatically, at just the right moment. You don't have to sit there sending emails yourself; you simply set it up once and it does all the hard ongoing work for you.

Infusionsoft can even send messages to your staff instructing them to post things to prospects and clients. The only downside is how difficult the software is to use... it's known as "Confusionsoft"! It's a powerful tool, but you need an expert to help get it set up for your practice.

Finally, you should also be collecting and keeping relevant information about clients. Every single contact with a client is an opportunity to help them while generating revenue... if you have information to leverage. In your practice you most likely have a client's individual attention for at least half an hour. That's your opportunity to build your relationship and find out how you can help them. You don't want to waste any of that time asking questions they have previously answered.

It might be that last time they had an appointment you talked to them about their lifestyle. You discovered they sat at a computer screen for eight hours a day, wore lenses during social occasions and loved swimming.

And here they are sitting in front of you again. Let's be honest, if it's the average client, they may look vaguely familiar, but you probably won't remember any details about them! Here's where a good information system is invaluable.

In our practice we record important information after every appointment. Not just their healthcare data, but information and observations about their lifestyle. Every morning the team huddles for 30 minutes to review the clients visiting that day. They can review the notes and remind themselves about the clients they saw last time.

If a client can't see the specific optician they saw last time, then the clinician seeing them can refer back to their last appointment, saying something like "Bob was telling me about your passion for swimming...".

This blows clients away! They realise they are dealing with a business that really cares about its clients.

A business with this kind of perception has a better relationship with its clients. A better relationship means they don't want to go anywhere else, and put their full trust in the hands of their optician. That's a business you can be proud of.

Grow your practice and sell it

9) Ensure your business thrives with operational excellence

If you're serious about growing your practice and selling it for the highest possible amount in the future, then the number one activity you should be spending time on is sales and marketing. The successful practice owner spends 50 to 80% of their time working on the business.

At the same time, it's also vital that you are operationally excellent in every way. **Your** clients need to be delighted with the service they get and the products they buy. This goes hand in hand with the premium service you should be delivering. Premium practices – the ones that attract the best clients – of course deliver the best service.

We've talked already about the need for excellent operational systems. You also need the best staff you can find to work the systems.

The best staff are ones that you can mould and develop. Always hire for mindset rather than ability. You can teach someone who thinks the right way how to perform a task. But you can't teach the right way to think, to someone who is good at a task.

Decide how you want your business to operate. Then give your staff a clear operations manual that lays out how you want things done. The simpler it is the better. An operations manual is not just something used by a systemised business such as a McDonalds franchise. The American small business guru Michael Gerber recommends using an operations manual to take control of your business, decreasing your stress and increasing your business's efficiency.

Implementing change while systemising a business can be a stressful thing in itself, especially if you have been running that practice for a while. You will find that your staff fall into two camps. Some will want to change – in fact they will be desperate for it – while others will have been with the practice for a long time and will have got far too comfortable.

The people who don't want to change are the ones that will hold your practice back. But the good news is, they will either change or leave. When you systemise a business for operational excellence, people who can't work within that will simply leave. It's nothing to be scared of.

Get all of this right and your business becomes significantly more sellable. More on this later.

10) Why you must stop seeing clients yourself, and lose some of them by increasing your prices

Changing and growing a business is a difficult journey. When you solve one set of problems, a new set always comes along. There is virtually never a point where your business doesn't demand attention in one area or another. In fact, the process of devoting significant attention to get one area sorted tends to allow problems to develop in another area.

But then, you knew that already.

Guess what the number one thing is that holds your business back? It's YOU! The business owner is normally the main obstacle to growth. You might not believe that's correct for your situation, but sorry – the chances are high that it is.

It certainly was in my business. I reached a point, about a year before we opened the second practice, where I was holding the business back so much it was scary. At the time I was really busy during the day seeing clients. I mistakenly thought my role was as the main revenue earner for the practice – because some clients want to see the most senior clinician, right?

I was packing the appointments in all day and then going home grumpy at night, as I still had all the other things to do. The finances, the marketing, the staff problems. My staff were very patient with me and they had to be. Anything they wanted me to look at always took so much time. They would suggest an idea to me and it would be a few days before I got round to looking at it.

I was a massive bottleneck to the business. These days it's not about big businesses beating small. It's about fast businesses beating slow. I was making my business a slow business. Everything went at my pace; the pace of an over busy man with no spare time.

Of course, this also created difficulties at home. No partner wants their other half to spend their time preoccupied with work. Or worse, spending the time at home feeling guilty about not working (and of course the time at work feeling guilty about not being at home!).

The answer came to me like a bolt out of the blue while I was on holiday (always take quality time away from your business. You will have a greater clarity of thinking). I had to stop seeing clients – immediately. Because as long as I was spending the majority of my working time seeing clients, the business would not be able to grow more quickly, and I would not achieve my rather ambitious goals.

Yes, it was a risk. There was always a chance that some of my clients would not accept an alternative optician and leave the practice. I think we lost a couple of stubborn people. But that was nothing compared to what the business gained.

You see, I can directly track the profitable opening of my second practice back to the decision I made on that holiday. And that's because I know now that the performance of your business is directly linked to **the way that you think and act.**

You need to be in a position where you can sit outside of your business and look at what's really happening. Things are constantly changing. The multiples are becoming more aggressive. The internet is making it easy for someone with a good idea to change an entire industry. You can no longer be set in your ways and continue to run your practice as it has always been run.

Who knows what will happen over the next decade? Personally, I'm excited, because change brings opportunity, and as someone who tries very hard not to get involved in the day-to-day running of the practice, I know I am perfectly positioned to see the change and react to it in the right way.

I still do some clinical practice (because I enjoy it) but I only deal with the practices' most important clients. Those who spend the most revenue and rightly, feel that they want to deal with the most senior person in the business.

Everyone else sees a member of my team, whose mind is fully on the job, meaning they probably deliver a better, less rushed service than I used to.

I realised a while ago that if you were able to hire and train the perfect optician, then fill every single appointment they had available, you would get a half a million pound return on your investment of approximately £45,000 a year. Now that's a great business!

Even if you only filled half their appointments, they would generate a quarter of a million pounds worth of business. It simply doesn't make sense for you to see lots of clients. You're worth more to your practice as the business owner than as a clinician.

How do you get started? Get a locum in for a couple of days a week. Invest the money in generating time for yourself. Spend the time you generate working on your business. You can't do that inside the practice of course... find a local coffee shop and work from there. It will seem odd at first, but you'll soon learn to enjoy growing your business over coffee and cakes.

One quick note on putting your prices up – just do it. Don't worry about it so much. Your best clients aren't as price sensitive as you think. Nudge your prices up once a year. Not too much, just enough to see a small rise in revenues. The cost of running the practice rises every year, right? You need to pass the cost on. The few clients who even notice let alone complain are never going to be great clients.

And this is the one time when you should ignore what your staff say. Remember, they are at the coalface dealing with the complaints, and will lose perspective that one person in 500 whinging about increased prices is nothing to be too worried about. Plus your staff will tend to judge the cost of treatment and frames on their own inability or unwillingness to pay!

11) Create a highly positive cash flow

The number one way for a business to die is for it to run out of cash. You can have a profitable business, but if you have more bills to pay than available money, then the business can't continue trading.

Running a practice is not cheap. It costs money just to be open for business every day. Payroll has to be met each **month** and bills paid no matter how many or few clients you have seen.

One of the biggest cash drains you will face – and especially if you take my advice to sell a number of premium brands – is stocking frames. So I suggest you negotiate with your suppliers either an extended payback period or an exchange policy.

And if you haven't got that in place then you're with the wrong suppliers. I have a standing instruction that sits with my practice managers. When new frame companies want to come on board, then they have to agree to a 90 day payment period or one-for-one stock exchange. Otherwise we simply will not stock their frames.

Why would suppliers accept this? Well, it works to their benefit too. If they're rotating your stock, you've always got the latest frames and no dead stock.

When it comes to selling frames to clients, you need to ensure they help your cash flow and don't hinder it. Why do clients go shopping to supermarkets carrying money to pay for their goods before they leave, but visit the opticians without the ability to pay for their new glasses!

At our practices we insist on a 50% deposit before we order frames. This is non-refundable so you've immediately covered the cost of the product, no matter whether they go on to pay the rest or not.

Interestingly, what you often find is that your best clients – the ones who have a great relationship with you – are more likely to simply pay the full amount up front. Brilliant! You have the products paid for before you've even ordered them.

I get so frustrated when I see a practice telling clients they can "get the payment sorted when they come to pick up their glasses". Not only does it introduce the risk of the client not paying, but it's a cash flow killer.

What do you do about those people who won't pay their deposit? You give your staff a helpful excuse to fall back on. They can tell the client that the computer system won't allow them to place a manufacturing order until the deposit has been paid.

Clients will take your lead. If it's standard practice behaviour to ask for a 50% deposit, that's what people will do. It doesn't matter what your competitors do. You need to do what's right for your business.

12) Prepare your business for a highly profitable exit

Every business owner leaves their business at some point. They either die, or it goes bust, or they sell it. Obviously, you want it to be the last option!

I'm sure you have in mind an exit one day. Even if you don't know the details or the timings, you need a clear exit strategy to focus the decisions you make along the way.

For example, if you know that your plan is to sell your practice to one of your opticians, then that should heavily affect the people you choose to work with right now. The people you hire today need to be able to step up to the mark in the future and buy the practice from you.

If that is your plan, it could be very helpful to make this a part of your recruitment process right from the start. Your staff will be more engaged in what they are doing and more keen to grow the business if they know that one day they will have an option to buy it.

And you will get more money for it. The practice owner with a clear exit strategy, who works hand in hand with the person they are eventually going to sell the business to, typically sells their business for a higher price.

There are a number of things that buyers and their professional advisors look for. They need to know that the business can operate without you – in fact, a lot of the things we have already talked about such as systemising your business and putting in place an operations manual will make it more valuable.

A positive cash flow is appealing as it will help the new owner get a return on investment more quickly. And if you can demonstrate growth in both turnover and profits over a number of years you will get a better offer.

One mistake made by many opticians is to hang on to their practice for too long. The best time to sell is while you are still passionate about the business and enjoy working on it. You can tell when the owner of a practice has fallen out of love with it. And that's a shame, as it ironically becomes harder to sell.

What to do next

So there they are, the 12 critical areas to focus on to create a practice that you truly love.

You can have a business that requires you to work less, have fewer clients and gives you less stress – yet makes you significantly more money over the next 12 months.

Looking back at the last 10 years and writing this book has been an interesting exercise for me. One thing I haven't touched on is how many mistakes I made along the way.

My goodness, I have got some things terribly wrong! For every good idea there have been five rotten ones that wasted time and cost money! But of course I learnt from them; kept my focus; and never, ever lost sight of what I wanted to achieve.

To do that I surrounded myself with positive, knowledgeable people who I could learn from, and who could help me implement the specific changes I needed to make – quickly.

In this book I have only been able to touch on the problems that need to be addressed within your practice and how you actually go about doing that. And that's why my colleague Paul Green and I are putting on a free business growth and marketing seminar specifically for opticians.

You see, we have so much we would like to show you about how to improve and grow your practice over the next 12 months.

The seminar is free because it's a great way for us to meet a number of opticians in one place. Some of those then choose to go on to work with

Paul and I, and the other experts involved with Independent Practice Growth UK.

I'd like to personally invite you to attend a seminar. To see the latest dates, read the full details and secure your free place, go to **www.practicegrowthseminar.co.uk**

Good luck developing your practice. I hope to meet you at a seminar soon.

Yours,

Richard Pakey

Richard Pakey
Owner of two independent opticians practices
And founder of Independent Practice Growth UK

Independent Practice Growth UK recommends these partners

specscare
Spectacle Insurance made easy

PERFORMANCE FINANCE
Unleashing your capital's potential
www.performancefinance.co.uk

PERFORMANCE INSURANCE
Where peace of mind costs less
www.performanceinsurance.com